Piet Paris
Fashion Illustrations

Heart and Hand
Introduction by Laird Borrelli

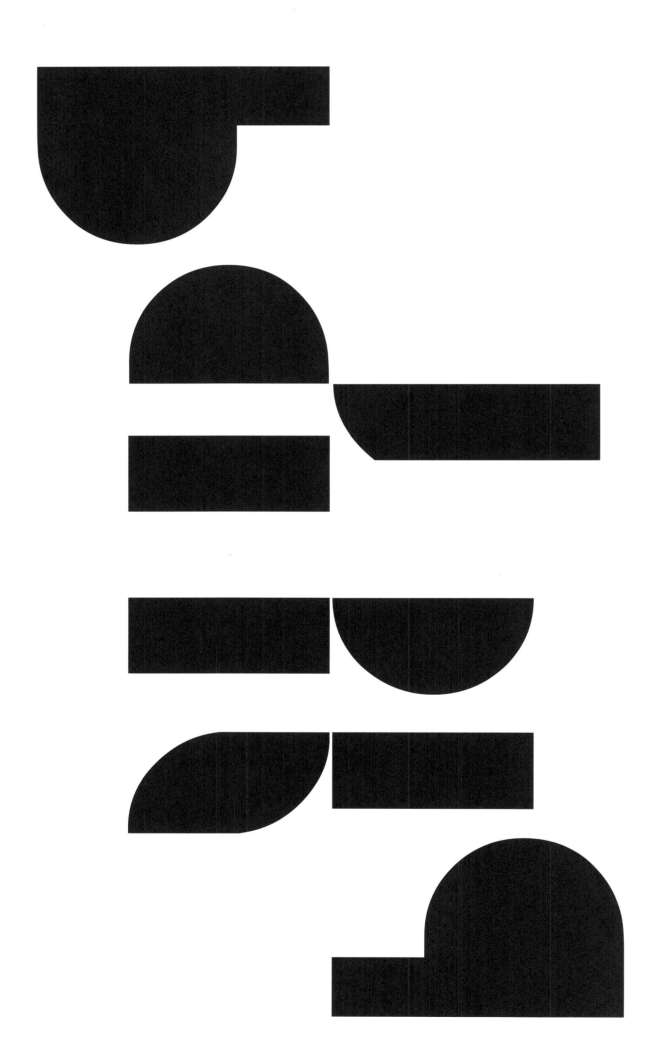

# Heart and Hand

All of the work in this book started the same way, with a blank piece of paper, a pencil, a light box – and the incomparable Piet Paris.

'I start from nothing,' says Paris, who, like his favourite painter, Johannes Vermeer, works in a traditional way, from a central axis, which anchors the figure.

Always searching for the perfect line, Paris covers the paper with stroke after stroke, turning the paper again and again over the light so as to make each drawing as perfect on the front as on the back (which explains his mirrored P. P. signature). 'It takes ages to come to the perfect line; it's what takes the most energy and it's what gives me the most pleasure,' Paris admits.

In the process of working, Paris's white becomes a web of lines that, over time, are reduced and the paper becomes emptier and emptier as the artist converts fashion into pure shapes. 'If I'm illustrating an Yves Saint Laurent dress,' he says, 'I can't draw all the frills and ruching and buttons.'

Indeed, Paris's gift is to be able to stylize the frivolous. The decorative element in his works comes from colour, preferably primary, applied stencil-like to his finished black-and-white drawing by hand, roller, spray paint or white collage.

Like much inspired work, Paris's technique was hit on by happy accident. Paris, who studied design and illustration at the Arnhem Academy of Art, often became frustrated when he felt that his drawings didn't work as a whole. The solution? He started to cut the good parts out, away from the wrong ones. This led to the stencil technique, because when the good parts were removed, empty spaces – ready to be filled – were left.

It's easy to see Paris's work as being minimal – and indeed his goal is to achieve much with little – but in fact the work derives its power from the delicate balance between the figure and the free space, the tension between the outer line and what it contains.

'The outline has to do with the inside shape as well,' Paris notes.

'I think if I had grown up in Paris my illustrations would be different,' says the artist (whose chosen nom de plume winks at the City of Light, the birthplace of fashion). Though reluctant to make comparisons between his work and that of the artists he admires, Paris's acknowledged influences are Dutch: Dick Bruna, he of the graphic, one-line rabbit, and Fiep Westendorp, creator of the beloved Jip and Janneke. The silhouettes of these story-book Dutch children are abstracted by being coloured black. 'From Westendorp I got the idea of drawing faces in profile,' Paris grants.

Is there significance in the fact that Paris names two children's illustrators as inspiration? His mother tells us that Paris was drawing on the walls when he was still in the playpen. This might be a key to understanding Paris's work – for however sophisticated and bold it might be, it also possesses a childlike purity. 'I think for me, fashion is about shape,' Paris says.

Yet 20 years into his career he still has to explain what his job is, what illustration is, and rues the fact that there isn't a more grown-up approach to understanding the art. 'It's funny,' Paris muses, 'because everyone starts his life by making drawings. Children are encouraged to draw and their works are hung on the wall – and then if you make it your job, no one wants to understand anymore.'

Mature in his career – celebrated in the 110 artworks that follow – and confident in his technique, one nevertheless feels that Paris maintains the ardour of a child's brimming heart. He delights and lures us with images as irresistible as candy to a babe.

'Illustration is such a beautiful way of me telling about my all-time love affair – with fashion,' Paris admits. And so each of his artworks is presented to the world as a valentine.

Laird Borrelli

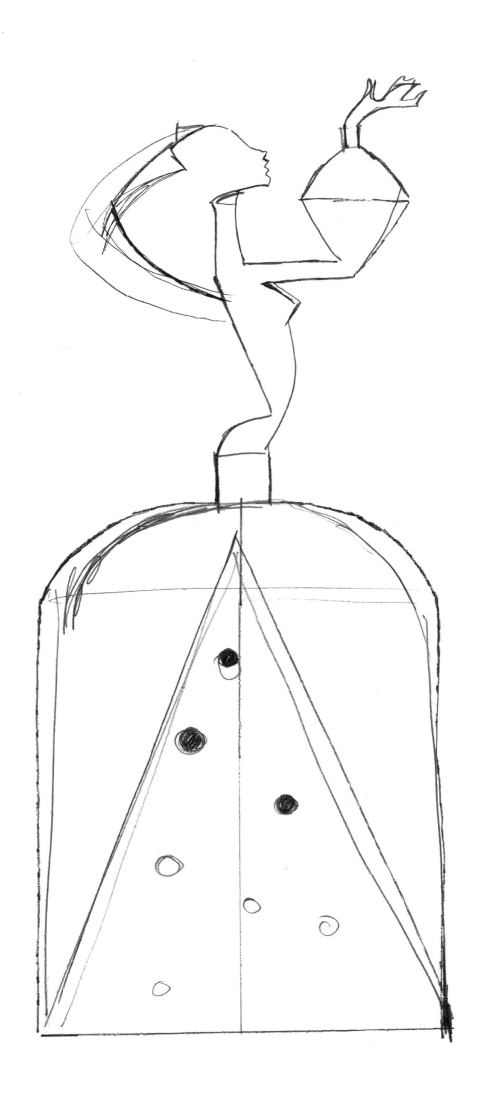

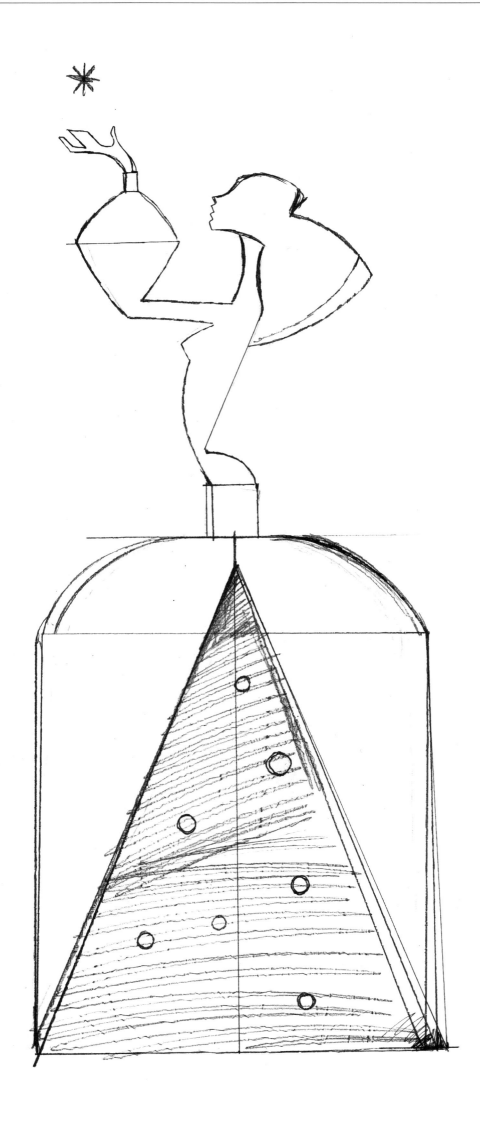

Cutting out sections of the sketch and filling the opening with paint. Stencils and paper shapes ensure crystal-clear delineation from the very first sketch. Easily legible and distinctly recognizable.
The delineated forms that result from the refined placement of stencils have become a trademark. They show up best when set against a white background.
The residual space is as important as the form itself.

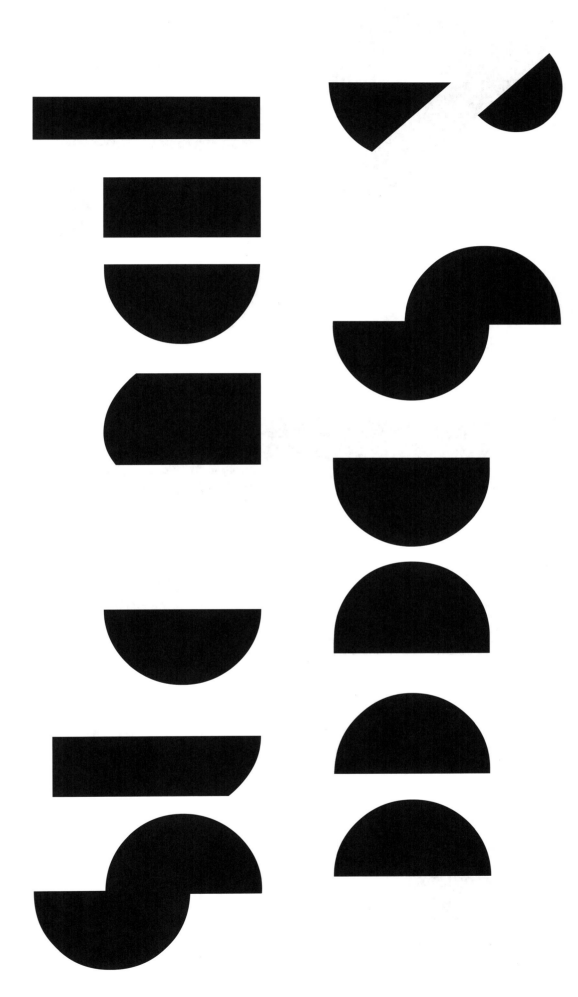

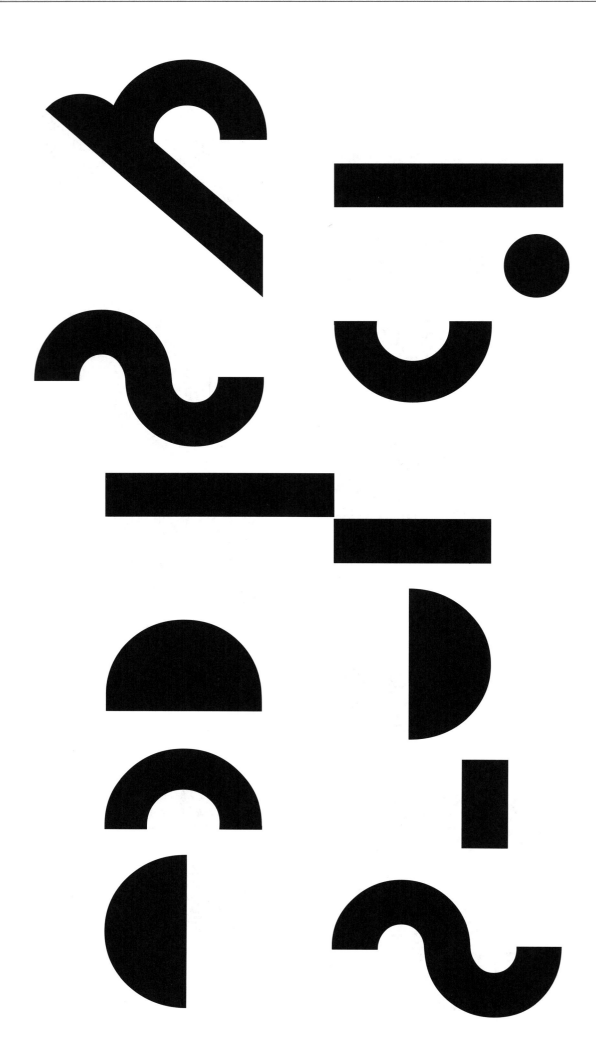

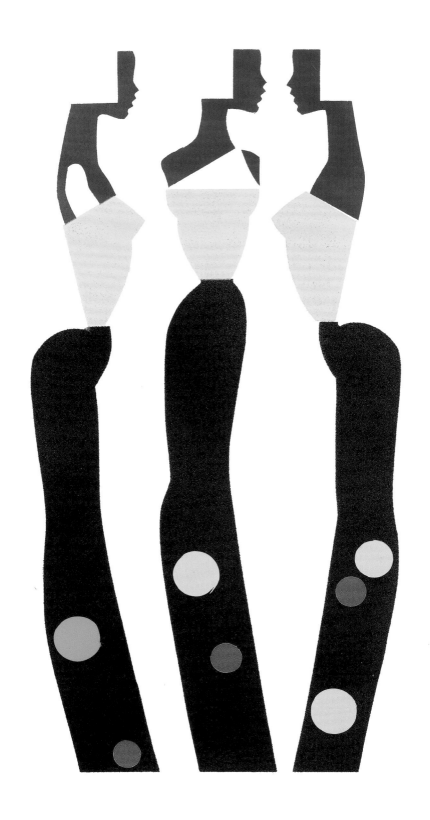

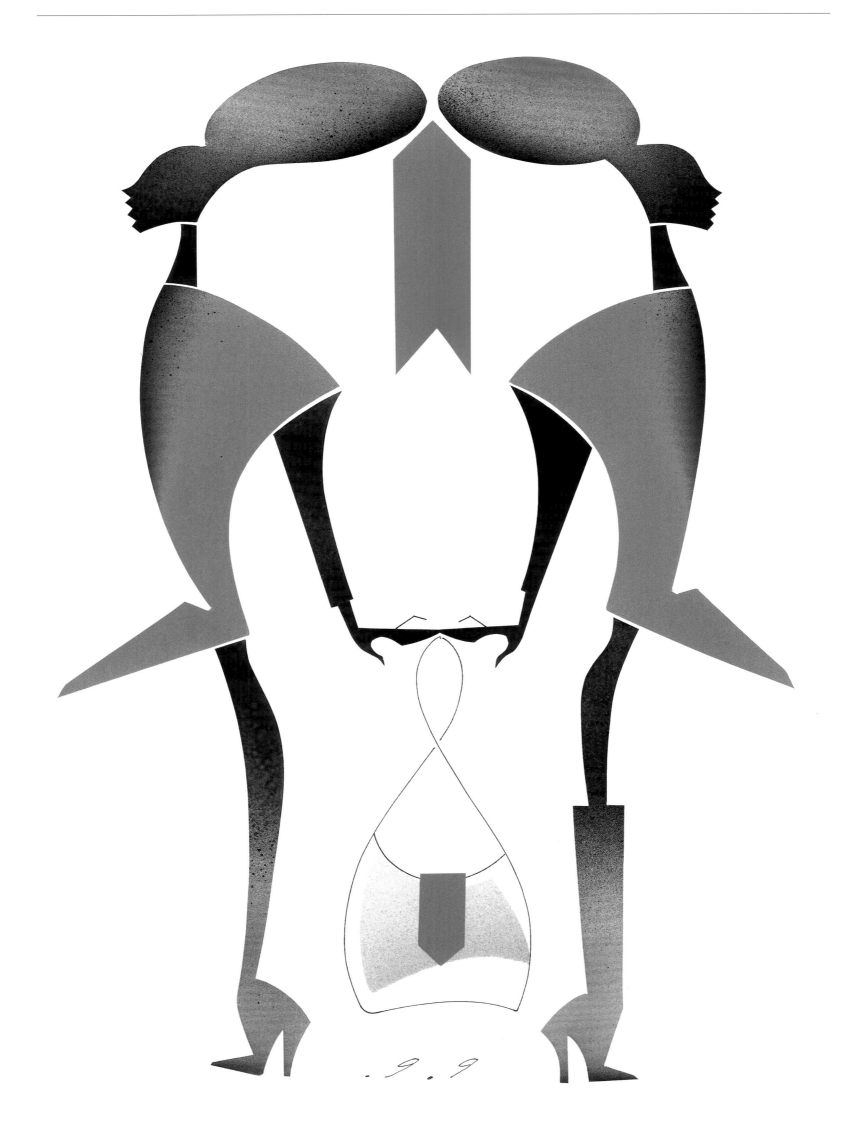

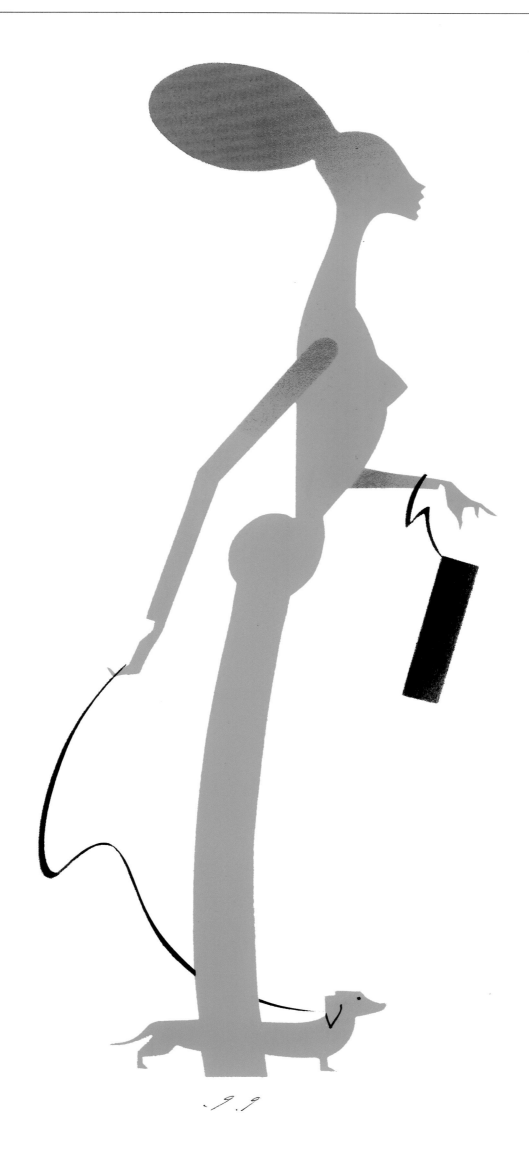

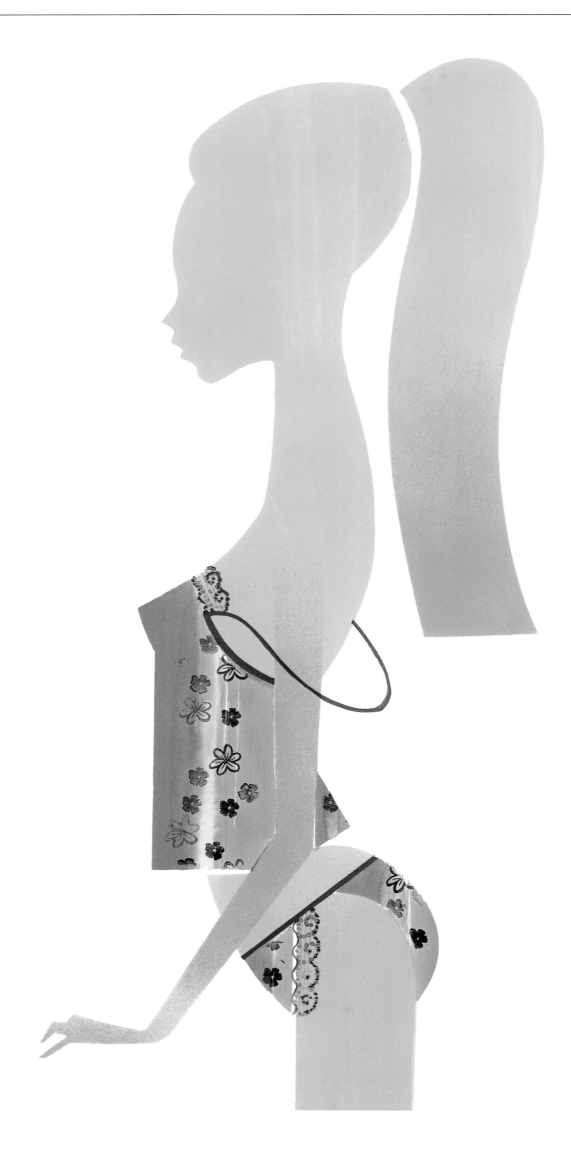

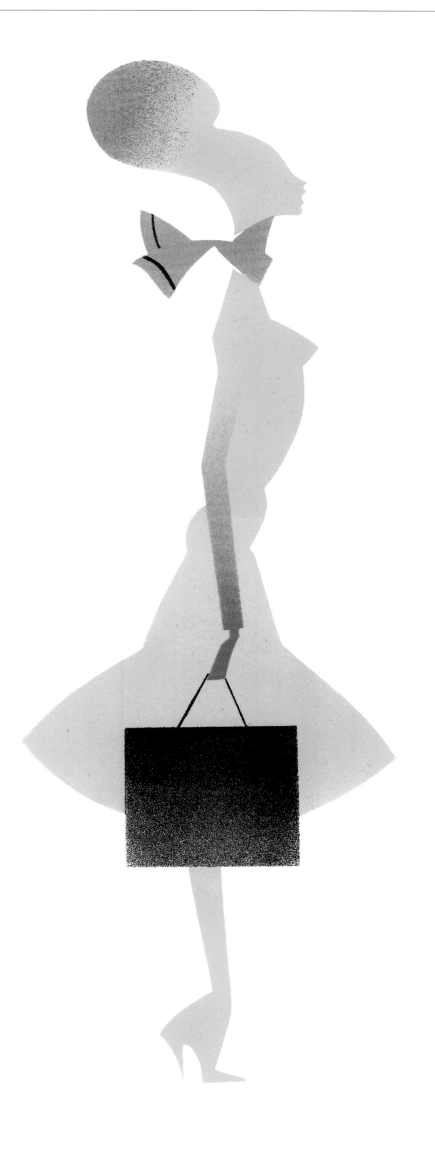

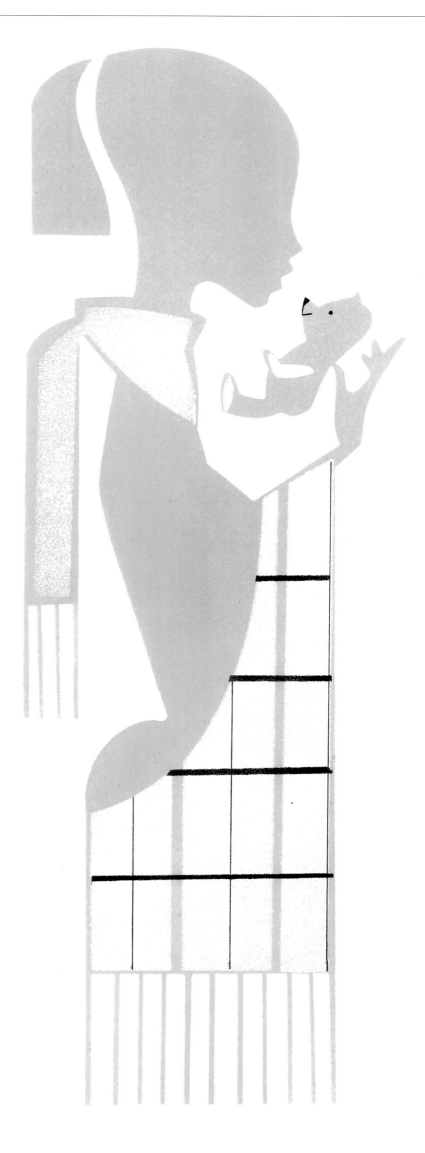

Fashion means progress and it doesn't linger in the past. Without the urge for innovation there would be no fashion, and in a drawing it is no different. The model moves and you witness a fashion moment: Where is she heading? What is she planning? A blink of an eye and it's all over, one more and she is towering above you.

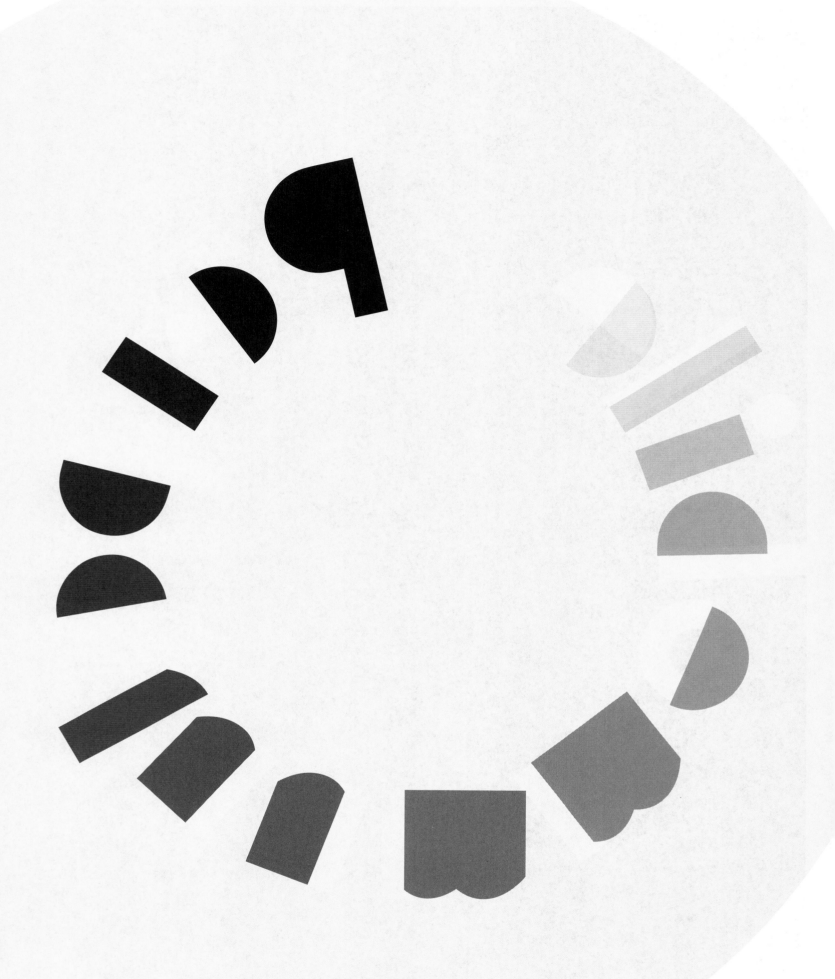

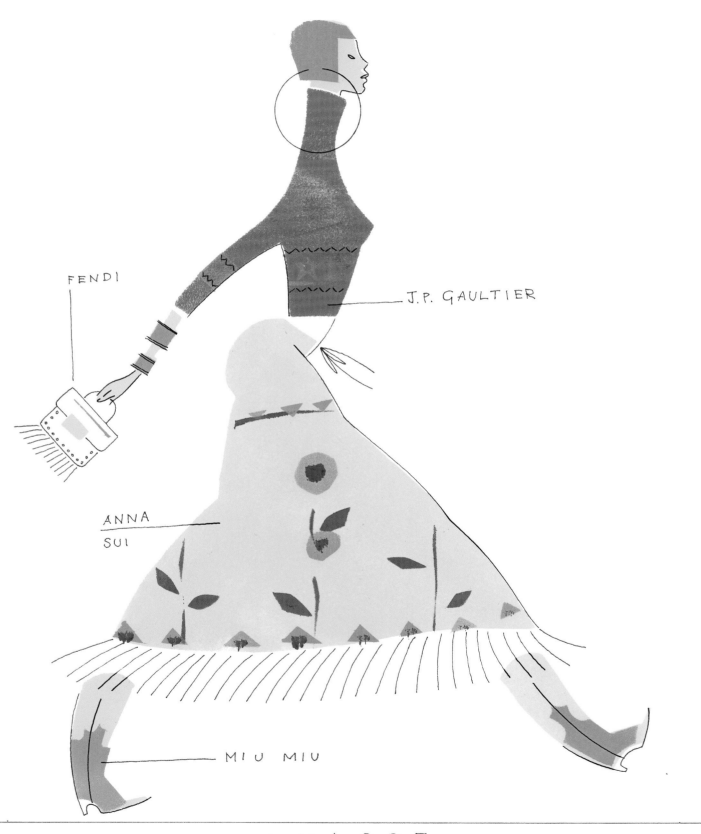

FENDI

J.P. GAULTIER

ANNA
SUI

MIU MIU

Full-blown drawings with animals
set alongside products. In adver-
torials, an advertisement presented
in an editorial format, the illustration serves the commercial
message. Plenty of backgrounds
and identical formal principles.
A black outline? Not around just
one of them, but around them all.
The full-length figures retain similar
proportions. Here the illustrations
are presented in a series of 8 to 10.

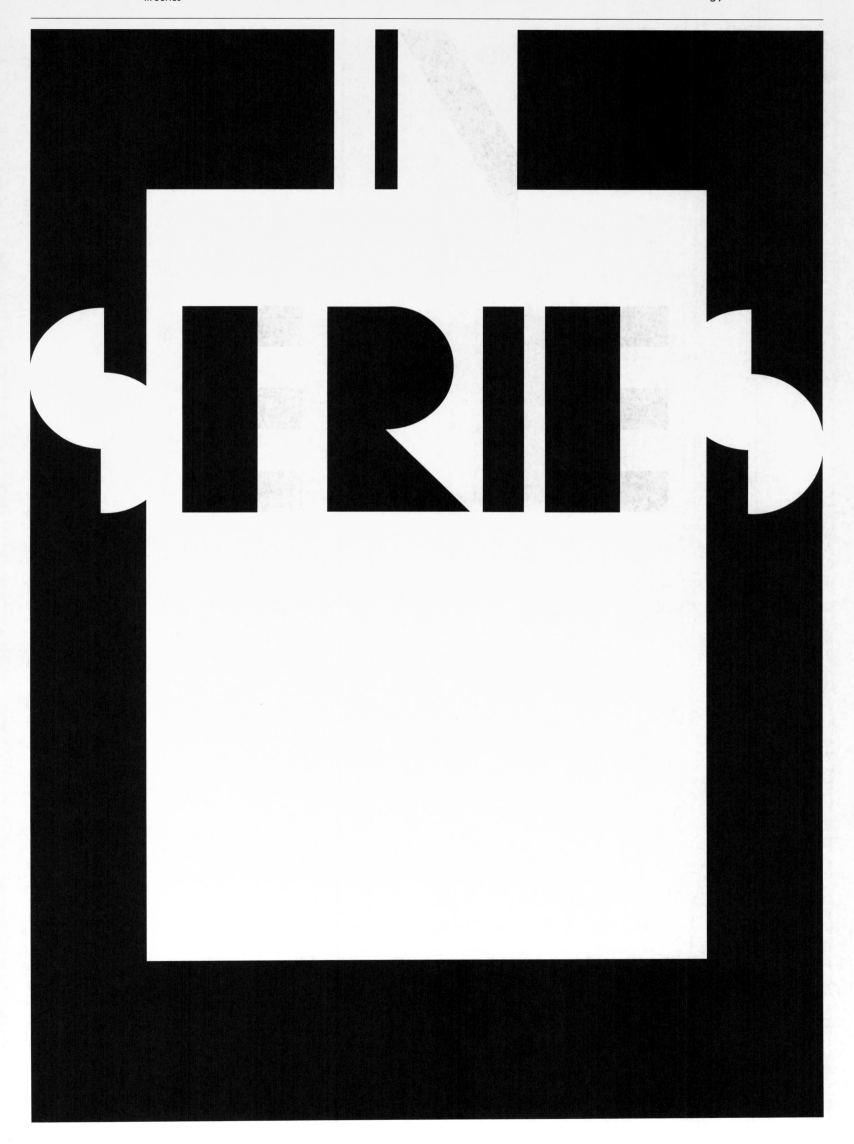

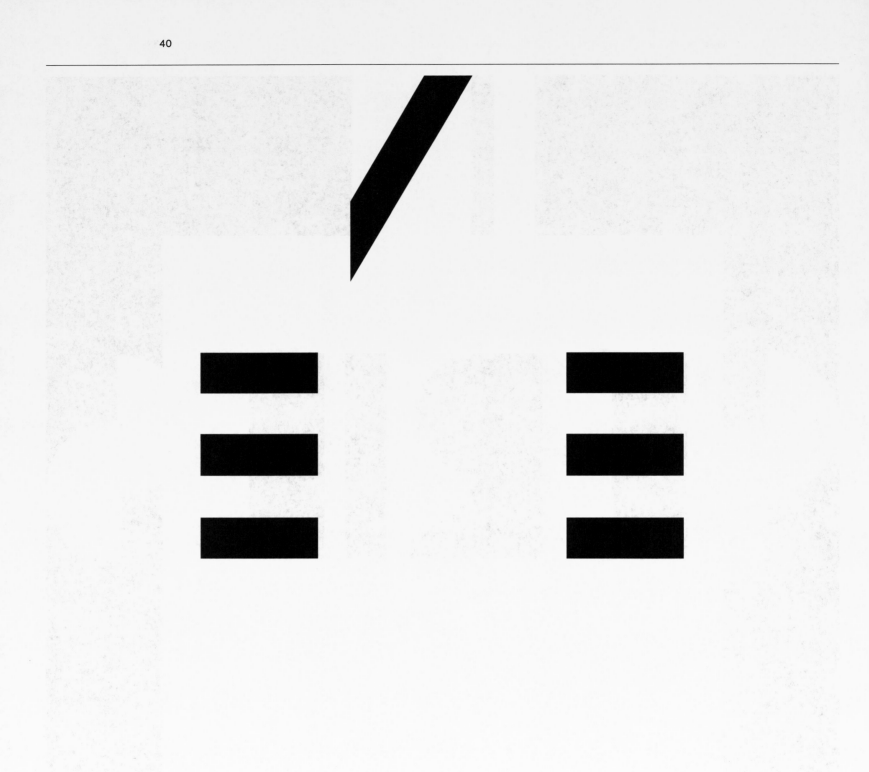

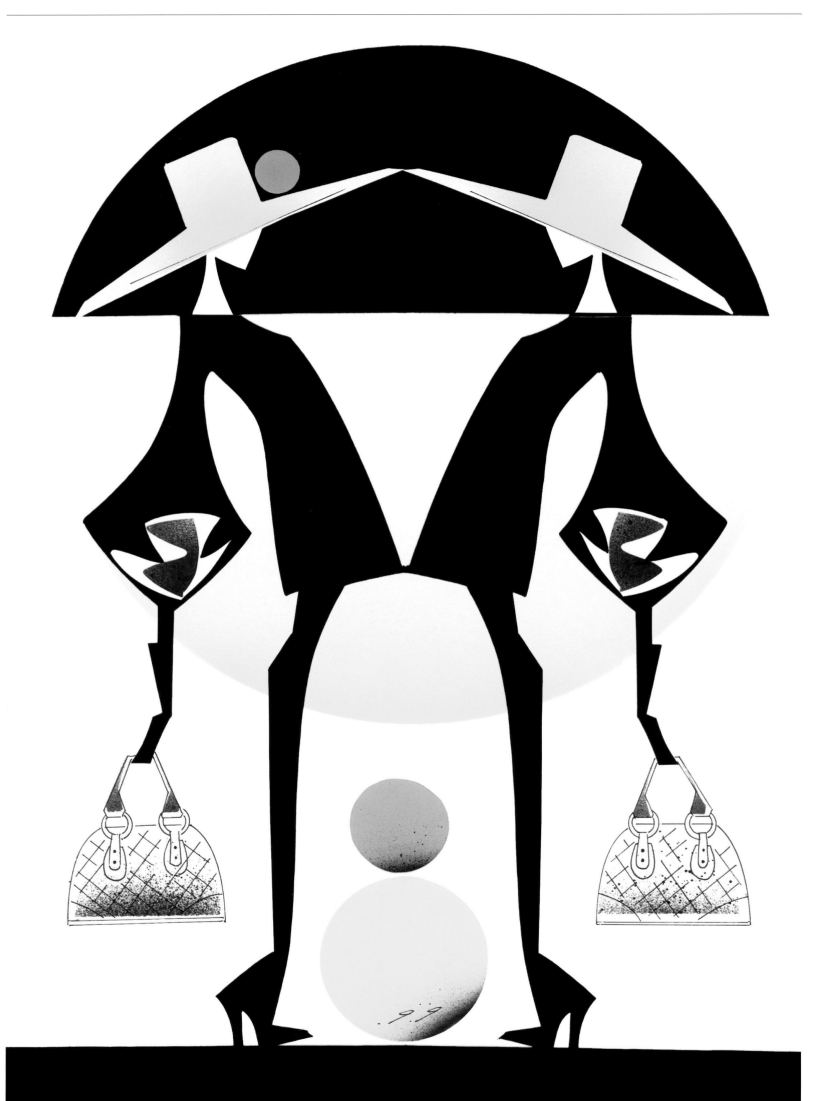

Hard, soft, thick and thin – working in pencil is the starting point for every illustration. And sometimes that first sketch turns out to be the final version. It is impossible to add any facets or introduce other stylistic devices. A web of lines has produced a fully fledged drawing.

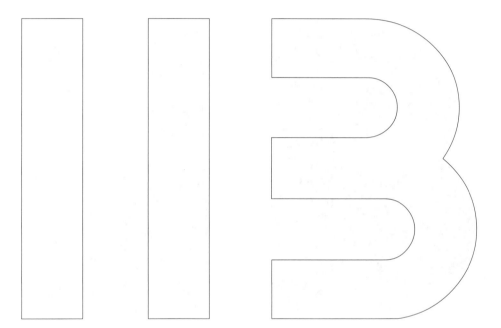

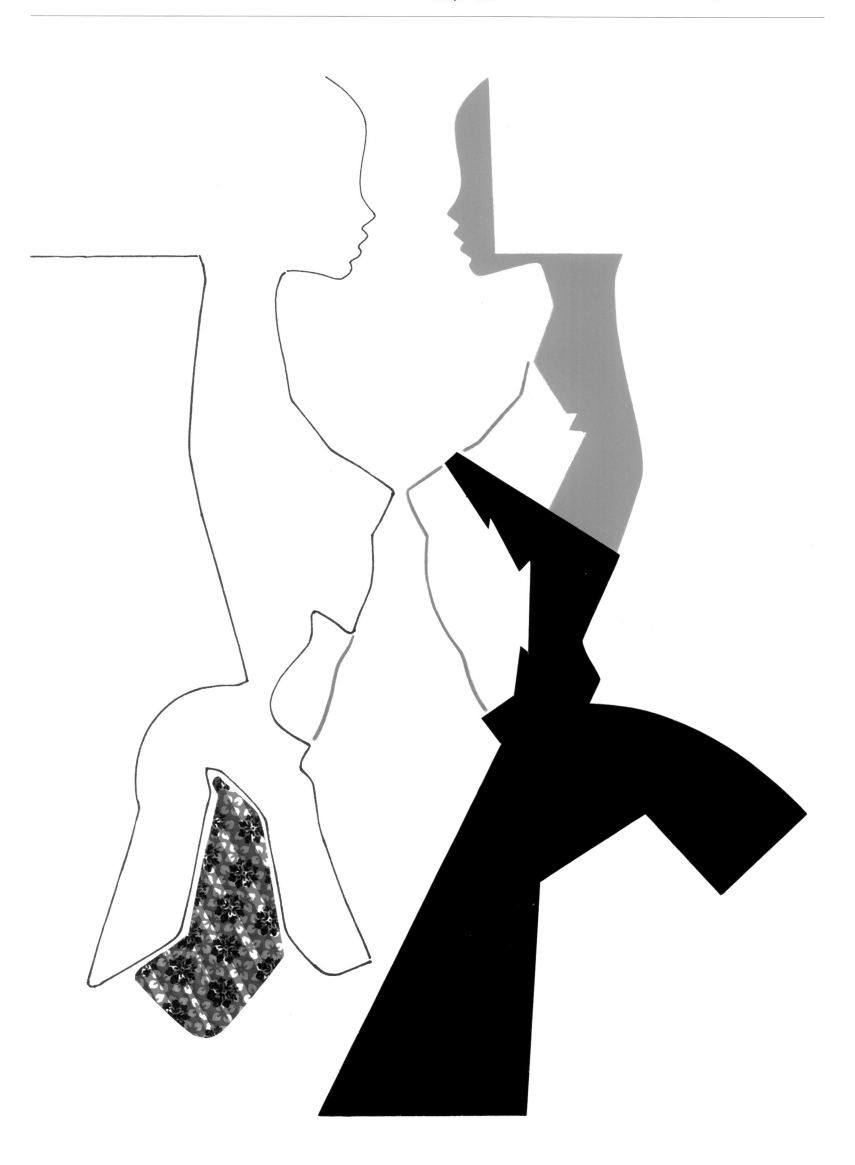

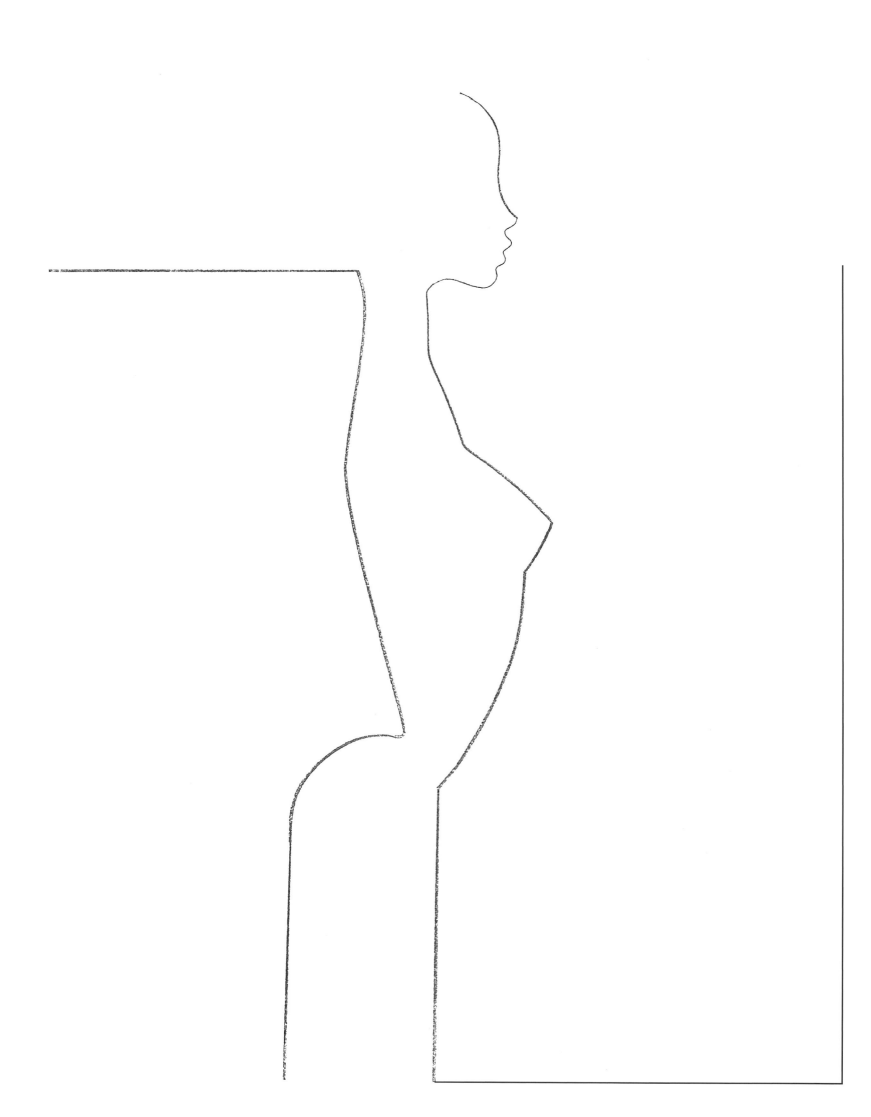

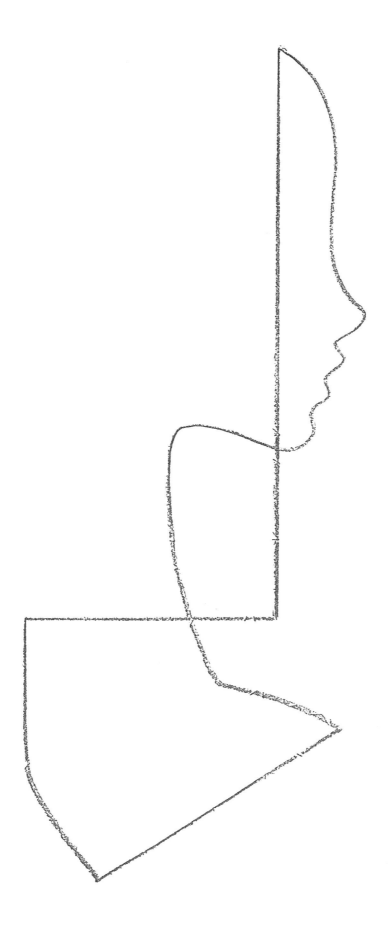

Fashion is a circle, a square, a triangle – or a building or a sofa. The client assigns and drafting begins. Illustrations created for corporate clients are crammed with information and appear in advertising campaigns and shop-windows, on bags and wrapping paper.

Teamwork is a prerequisite, whether sharing jotted ideas about the briefing or with a to and fro of e-mails: fine-tuning the shape of the eye, the swish of the dress or the dimensions of a bangle to achieve the perfectly detailed result.

He doesn't get very far, usually
just to the corner of the drawing.
For new forms, silhouettes, bags
and shoes, all attention is focused
on her. He extends his hand, opens
the door, starts the car and allows
her to shine without any fuss.
There's no escaping it: women
reign supreme in fashion.

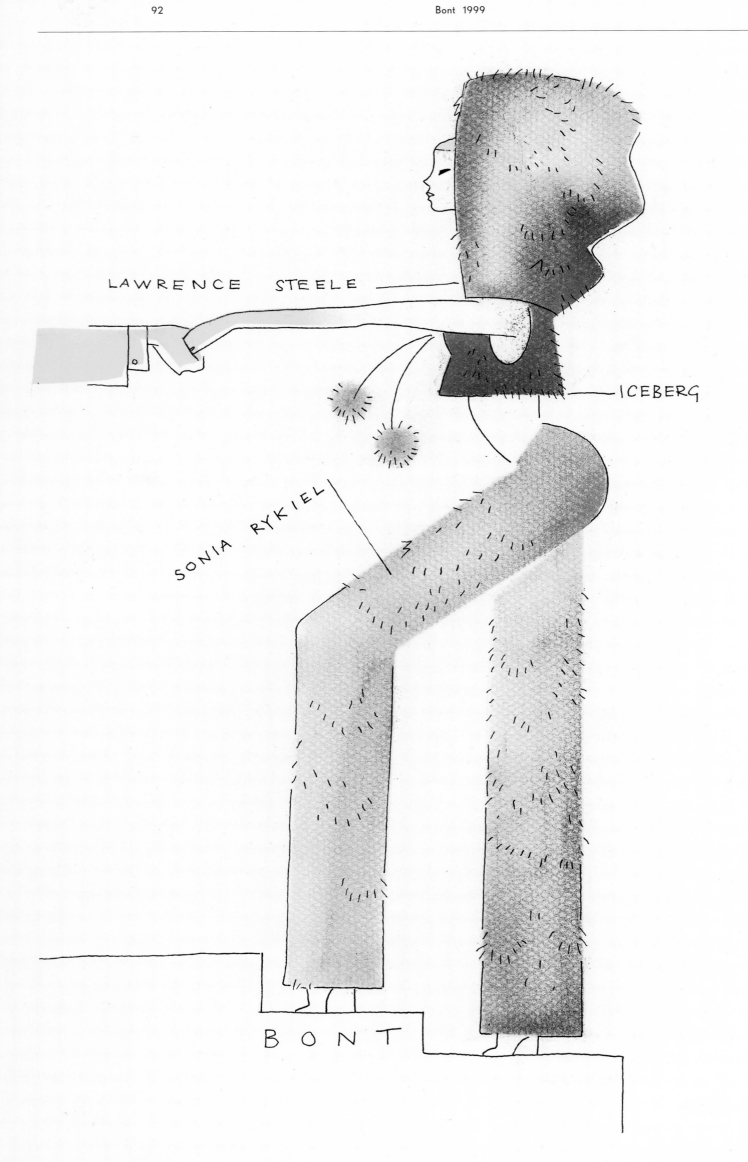

LAWRENCE STEELE

ICEBERG

SONIA RYKIEL

BONT

The simpler the better – these illustrations could even be used as posters. The function is what counts, and that is underscored by vigorous but simple stylization: primary colours rendered for the cover of a magazine, a composition that is not too busy but conveys an unequivocal message. December is for presents, and preferably lots of them.

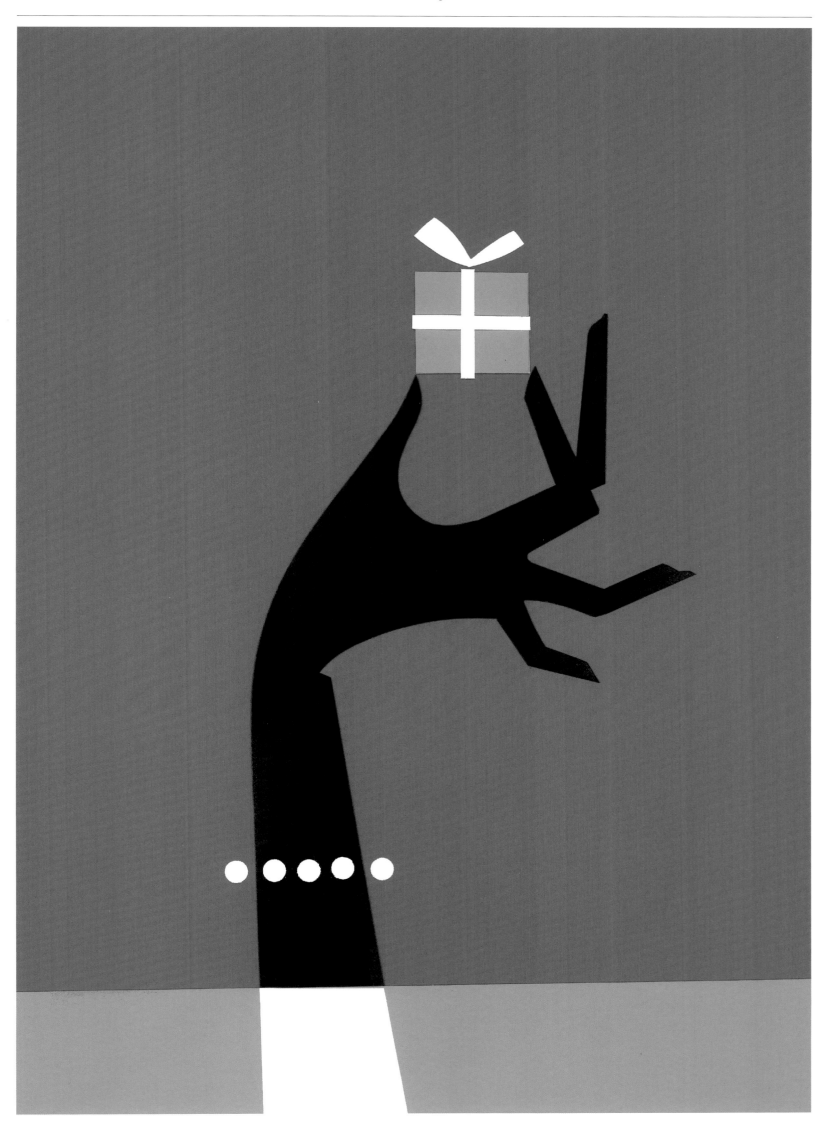

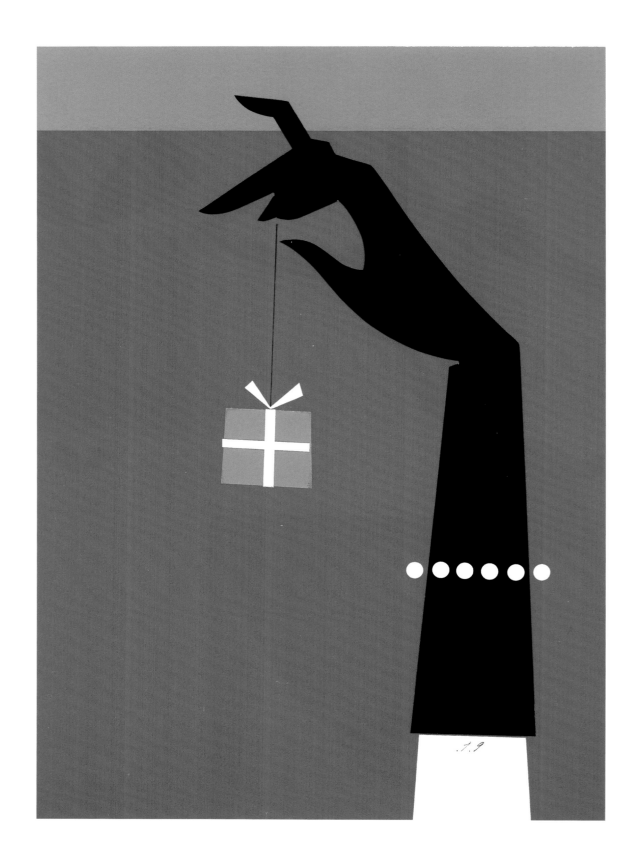

Here it is the ambience, as with movement elsewhere, that serves as the narrative device: it makes poetry of the portrayal. The figure in the illustration is active and casts her gaze skyward. She glimpses a falling star in an atmosphere reminiscent of Christmas: snow-flakes, a swirl of mist, a flurry of little feathers. Everything beautiful comes from above.

HEAV
ENLY
MESS
AGE

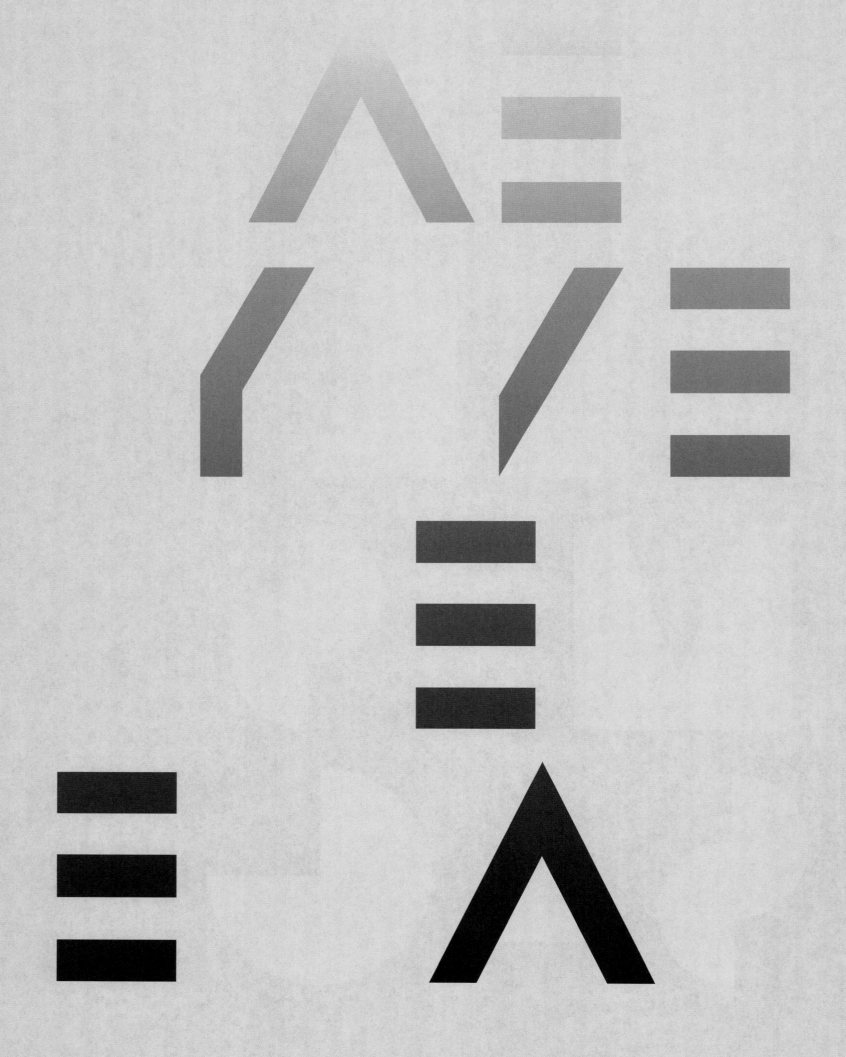

Frayed stripes to emulate shaggy woollen tweed. Strokes of poster-paint applied using a dryish boar-bristle brush to capture the texture of fur. Without textiles there is no fashion, and there is only one specific illustration technique which best captures that particular mobility and drape of the cloth. Illustrating fashion is about depicting the fabric, making manifest the expressiveness of textiles on a flat sheet of paper. A spray of paint for tulle brings the luxuriousness to life.

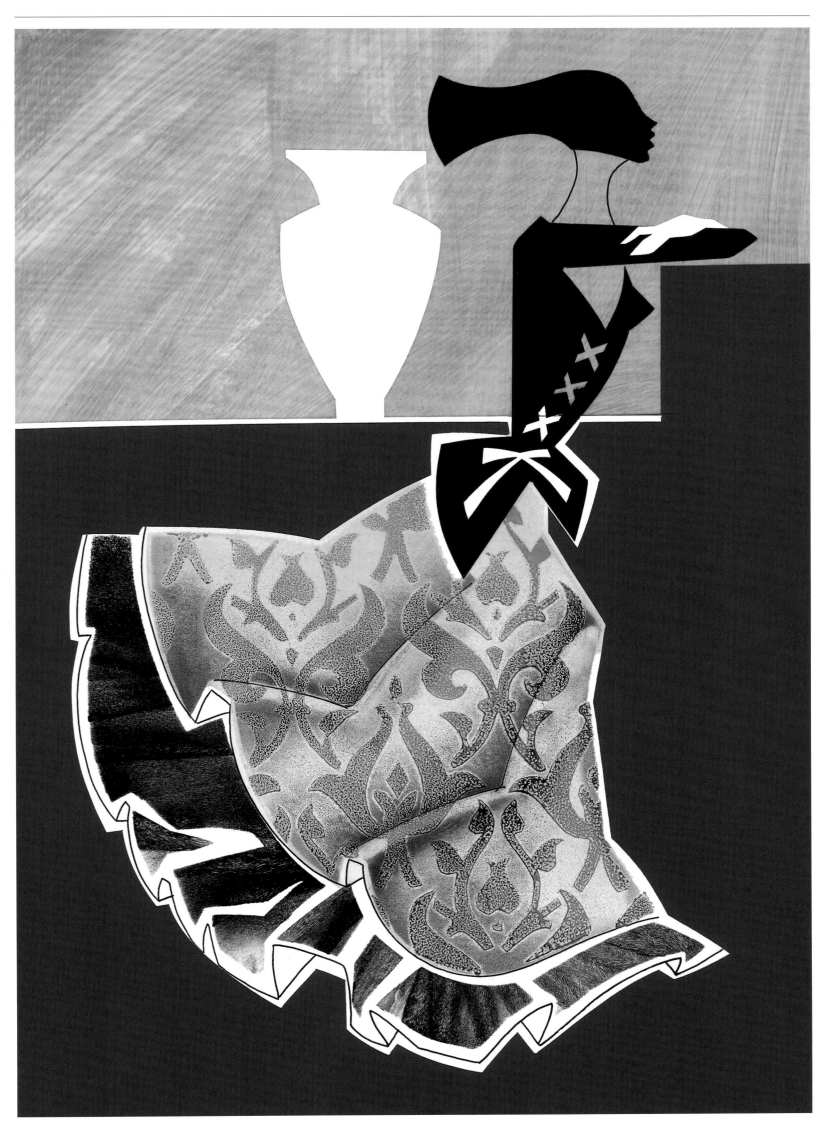

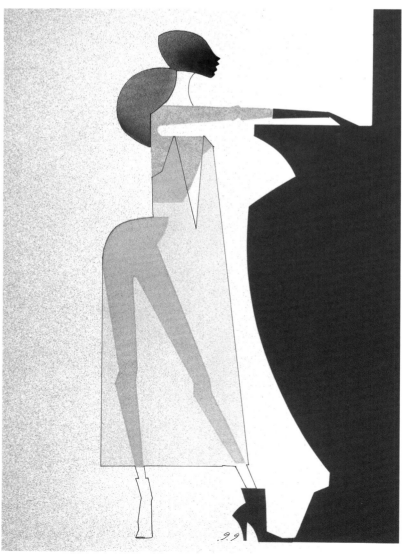

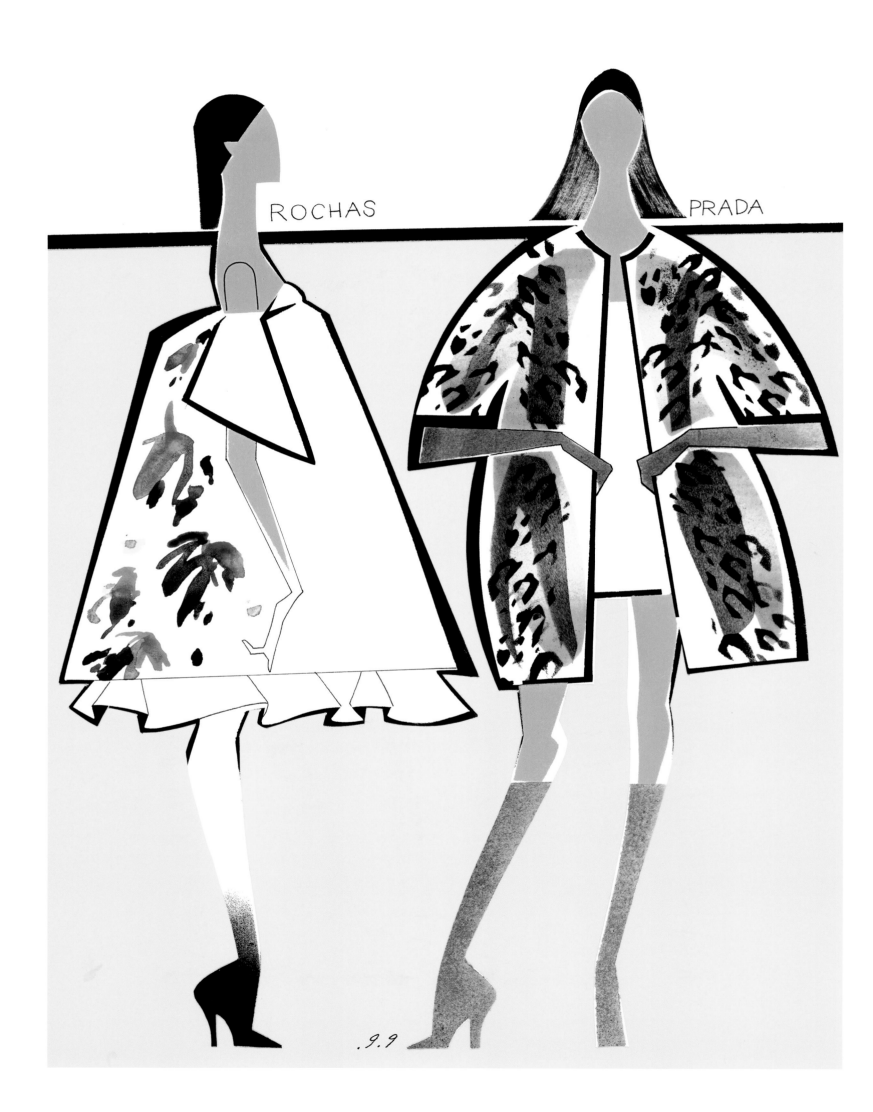

ROCHAS

PRADA

.9.9

As if hanging on a rail in a wardrobe or standing firmly on a plinth. The beam positions and fixes the graphic forms, whether supported or suspended. Having chosen to employ this idiosyncratic stylistic device, the elaboration proceeds well-nigh automatically. The mascara roller hangs like a clock and the model has both feet set firmly on the ground. With the top and bottom of the illustration now in balance the composition is resolved.

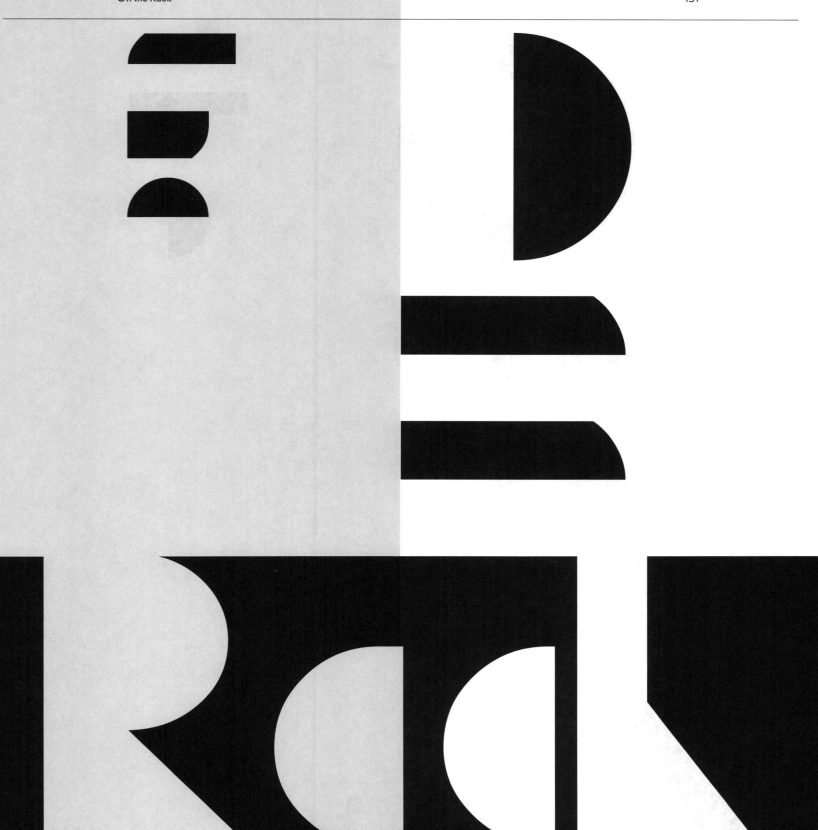

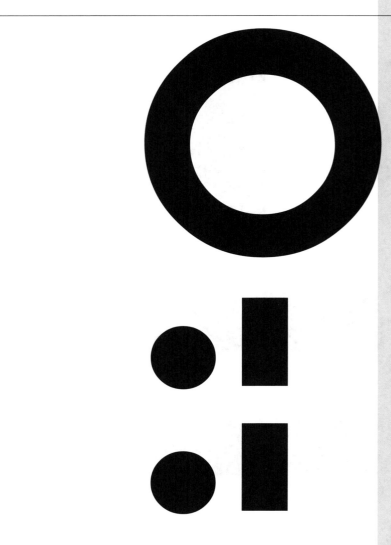

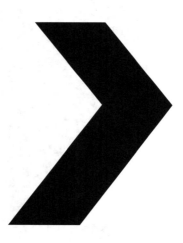

VOGUE

Thin paper lines interconnect
the components of the drawing.
To preserve the visual calm they
are often set horizontally. They
lend cohesion to the design, as
the beam does. Discovered while
experimenting, the line proved to
be practical as well as decorative,
because once the form has been
cut out from the paper the line
serves as a handy grip when
applying the adhesive to affix
the cut-out form.

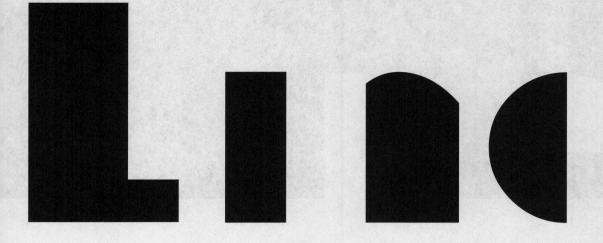

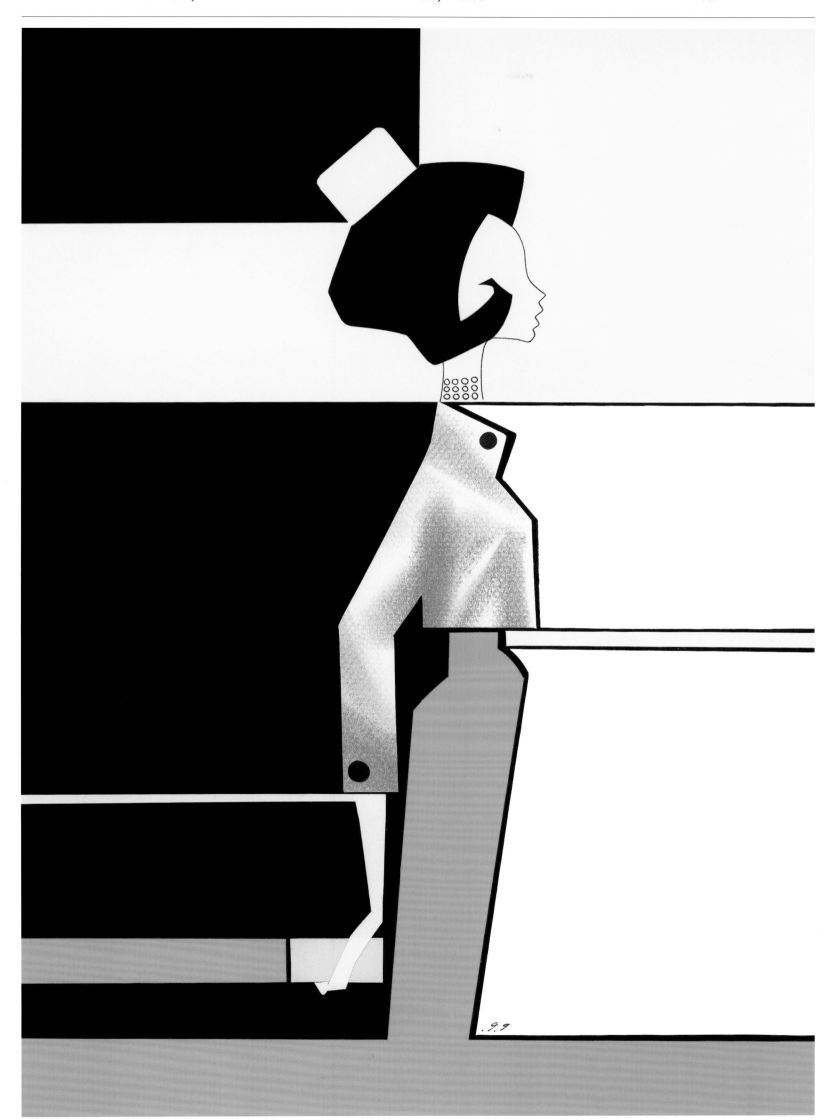

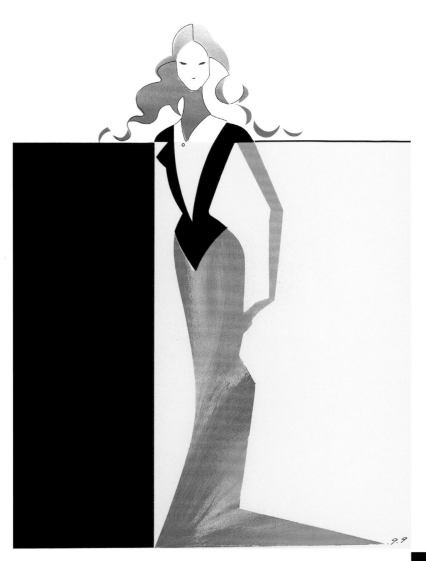

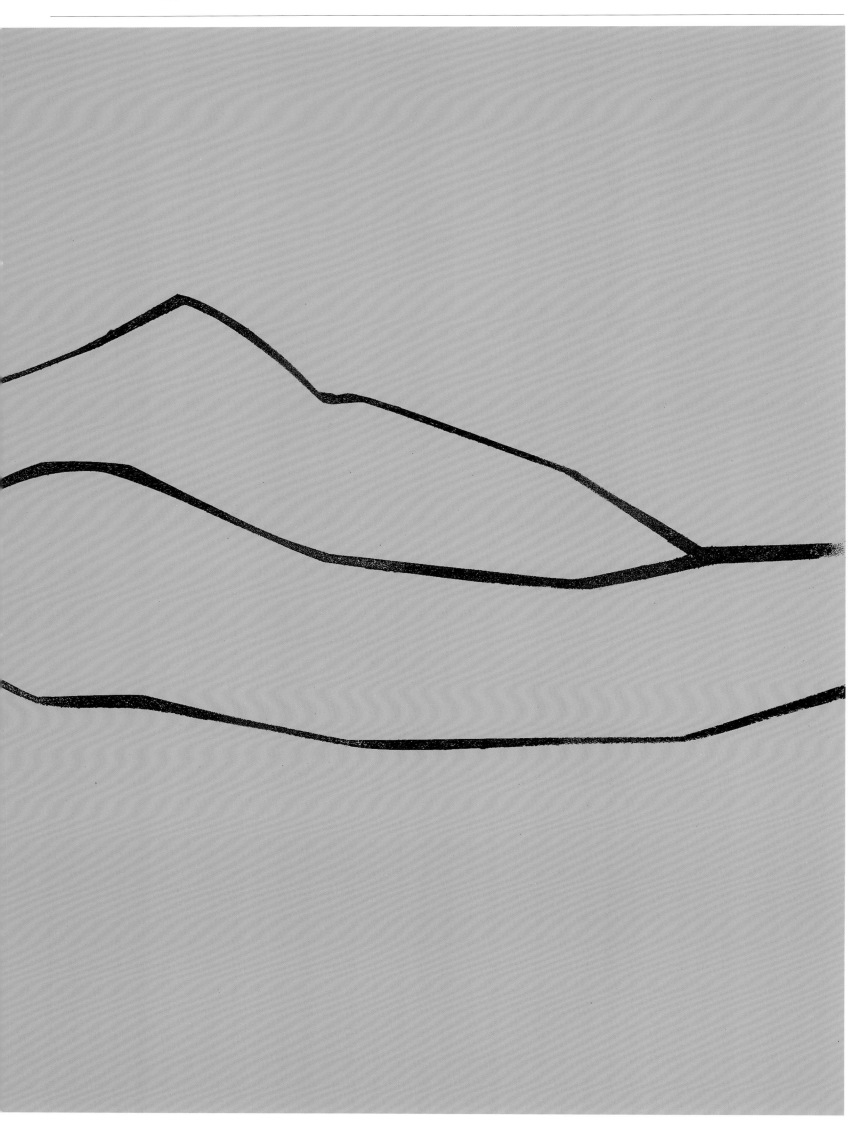

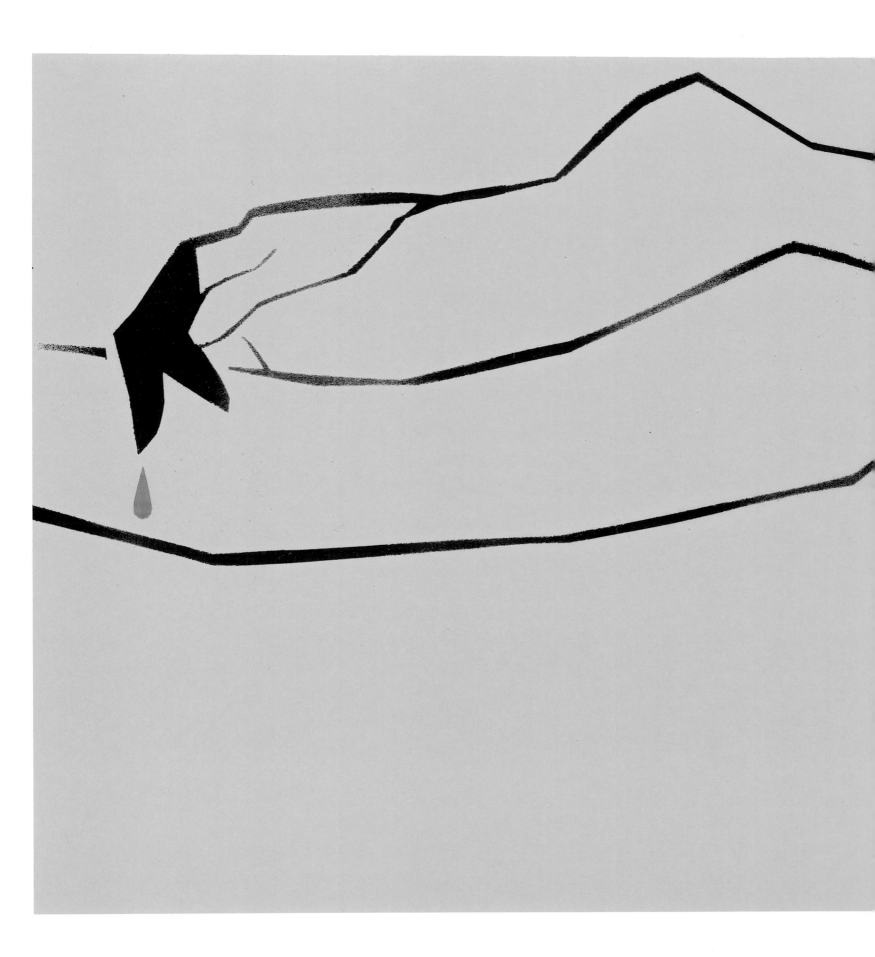

Original size of the illustrations is
A3, except for the illustrations
on pages 76 through 80 and 88.

All illlustrations by Piet Paris

Concept and graphic design
Coppens Alberts

Texts
Studio Piet Paris
Laird Borrelli

Translation
Andrew May

Publisher
WBOOKS
info  wbooks.com
www.wbooks.com

Print
EposPress, Zwolle

Lithography
Friedhelm Spickmann,
EposPress, Zwolle

Printed on Heaven 42  150 g/m$^2$ (Igepa)
and Dito 70 g/m$^2$ (Antalis)

Printed and bound in the Netherlands

ISBN: 978-90-89102-29-4

Copyright © 2011 by
Studio Piet Paris
www.pietparis.com

second edition, 2011

Piet Paris Illustrations is represented by
UNIT Creative Management Amsterdam
(Europe/USA) and by Art Liaison (Japan)